TENNESSEE
TITANS

BY JOSH ANDERSON

Stride

An Imprint of The Child's World®
childsworld.com

The Child's World®
childsworld.com

Published by The Child's World®
800-599-READ • www.childsworld.com

Photography Credits
Cover: © Andy Lyons / Staff / Getty Images; page 1: © Africa Studio / Shutterstock; page 3: © Frederick Breedon / Stringer / Getty Images; page 5: © Kathryn Riley / Stringer / Getty Images; page 6: © George Rose / Stringer / Getty Images; page 9: © Peter Aiken / Stringer / Getty Images; page 10: © Robin Alam/Icon Sportswire / Newscom; page 11: © stevezmina1 / Getty Images; page 12: © Andy Lyons / Staff / Getty Images; page 12: © Justin Berl / Stringer / Getty Images; page 13: © Mark Brown / Stringer / Getty Images; page 13: © John Sommers II / Stringer / Getty Images; page 14: © Wesley Hitt / Stringer / Getty Images; page 15: © Jamie Squire / Staff / Getty Images; page 16: © Al Bello / Staff / Getty Images; page 16: © Cliff Welch/Icon SMI / Newscom; page 17: © Andy Lyons / Staff / Getty Images; page 17: © Rob Tringali / SportsChrome / Newscom; page 18: © Rob Tringali / SportsChrome / Newscom; page 18: © Jonathan Daniel / Stringer / Getty Images; page 19: © Elsa / Staff / Getty Images; page 19: © Rob Carr / Staff / Getty Images; page 20: © Wesley Hitt / Stringer / Getty Images; page 20: © Andy Lyons / Staff / Getty Images; page 21: © Andy Lyons / Staff / Getty Images; page 21: © Andy Lyons / Staff / Getty Images; page 22: © Chuck Solomon/Icon SMI / Newscom; page 23: © Al Bello / Staff / Getty Images; page 23: © stevezmina1 / Getty Images; page 25: © Andy Lyons / Staff / Getty Images; page 26: © Joe Murphy / Stringer / Getty Images; page 29: © Doug Benc / Staff / Getty Images

ISBN Information
9781503857780 (Reinforced Library Binding)
9781503860681 (Portable Document Format)
9781503862043 (Online Multi-user eBook)
9781503863408 (Electronic Publication)

LCCN 2021952643

Printed in the United States of America

TABLE OF CONTENTS

GO TITANS!

The Tennessee Titans compete in the National Football **League's** (NFL's) American Football Conference (AFC). They play in the AFC South **division**, along with the Houston Texans, Indianapolis Colts, and Jacksonville Jaguars. While the Titans have never won a **Super Bowl**, they had winning records every season from 2016 to 2021. They have also made it to the **playoffs** 25 times, so fans hope that their team will win the big game soon! Let's learn more about the Titans!

AFC SOUTH DIVISION

Houston Texans

Indianapolis Colts

Jacksonville Jaguars

Tennessee Titans

FOLLOWING THE 2019 REGULAR SEASON, THE TITANS DEFEATED THE NEW ENGLAND PATRIOTS IN THE WILD CARD ROUND OF THE NFL PLAYOFFS 20-13.

BECOMING THE TITANS

The team now known as the Titans began playing in 1960, when they were called the Houston Oilers. They were part of the American Football League (AFL). The Oilers won the AFL Championship during the league's first two seasons in 1960 and 1961. They became part of the NFL when the two leagues merged just before the 1970 season. The team played in Houston, Texas, until the 1997 season, when the Oilers moved to Tennessee. Since 1999, they've been called the Tennessee Titans and play their home games in Nashville, Tennessee.

LEGENDARY PRO BOWL QUARTERBACK ARCHIE MANNING JOINED THE HOUSTON OILERS FOR TWO SEASONS LATE IN HIS CAREER.

BY THE NUMBERS

The Titans have played in **ONE** Super Bowl.

11 division titles for the Titans

513 points scored in 1961—a team record!

13 wins for the Titans in 2008

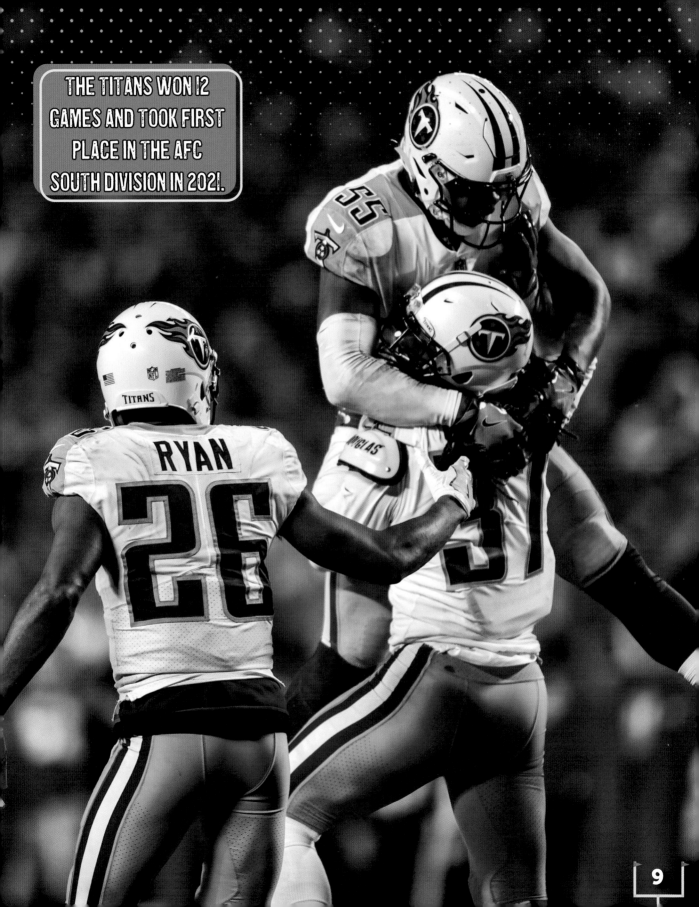

THE TITANS WON 12 GAMES AND TOOK FIRST PLACE IN THE AFC SOUTH DIVISION IN 2021.

FANS SHOWED UP IN RECORD NUMBERS IN OCTOBER 2021 TO WATCH THE TITANS UPSET THE BUFFALO BILLS 34-31.

In their early days, when they were the Houston Oilers, the team played in several different **stadiums**. For nearly 30 of those years, they played in the Houston Astrodome. The Astrodome was the world's first domed, air-conditioned indoor stadium. In 1999, they moved into their current home in Tennessee, Nissan Stadium. Nissan Stadium can hold about 69,000 fans on Titans game days. The Titans share the building with the Tennessee State Tigers college football team.

We're Famous!

In the 2000 movie *Cast Away*, a character played by actor Tom Hanks gets stuck on an island in 1995. His character lives in Tennessee. He manages to survive on the island for several years until he's rescued. When he's reunited with his girlfriend, she tells him the Titans lost in the Super Bowl to the St. Louis Rams. Since the Tennessee Titans were called the Oilers until 1999, he replies by asking, "We have a pro football team now?"

UNIFORM

BLUE

WHITE

Truly Weird

A normal NFL game takes a little more than three hours to finish. But the Titans played a game against the Dolphins in September 2018 that went a lot longer! Because of lightning in the Miami area, the game had to be stopped two different times to ensure the safety of players and fans. With all the weather delays, the game didn't finish until seven hours and eight minutes after it began. That's the longest game in NFL history!

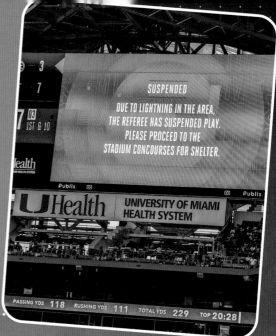

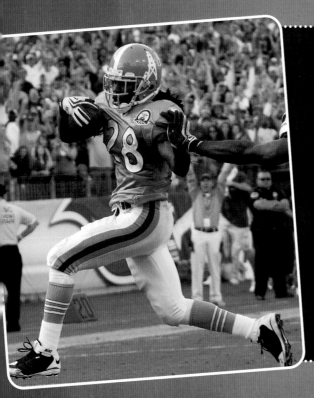

Alternate Jersey

Sometimes teams wear an alternate jersey that is different from their home and away jerseys. It might be a bright color or have a unique theme. The 50th anniversary of the AFL's founding was in 2009. To celebrate, the Titans wore "throwback" Houston Oilers uniforms for a few games that season.

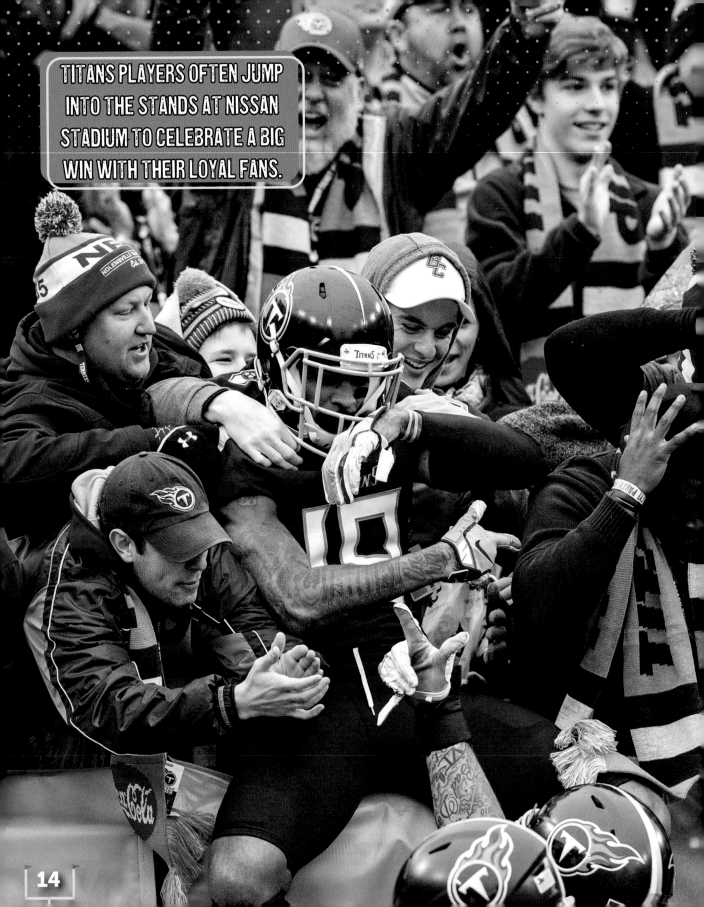

TITANS PLAYERS OFTEN JUMP INTO THE STANDS AT NISSAN STADIUM TO CELEBRATE A BIG WIN WITH THEIR LOYAL FANS.

TEAM SPIRIT

Going to a game at Nissan Stadium can be a ton of fun! Whether it's at a huge tailgate party before the game, or inside the building, fans yell, "Titan Up!" to cheer on their team! The Tennessee Titans Cheerleaders entertain fans during breaks in the action and at halftime. There's also the Blue Crew Drumline, which brings their unique beat to fans inside and outside the stadium. The Titans' mascot is T-Rac, a giant costumed raccoon who loves to pull for the team. The raccoon is the state animal of Tennessee.

T-RAC

HEROES OF HISTORY

Eddie George
Running Back | 1996–2003

George rushed for more than 1,000 yards in seven of his eight seasons with the team. His 10,009 rushing yards are the most in Titans history. George was selected for the **Pro Bowl** four times. After his playing career, George pursued an acting career and even earned a role in the Broadway production of *Chicago*.

Bruce Matthews
Offensive Lineman | 1983–2001

Matthews played all 19 of his NFL seasons in Houston and Tennessee. Between 1988 and 2001, he was selected for the Pro Bowl 14-straight times. In 2007, Matthews was inducted into the Pro Football **Hall of Fame**. He was also chosen as a member of the NFL's 100th Anniversary All-Time Team.

Steve McNair
Quarterback | 1995–2005

McNair led the Titans to the team's only Super Bowl appearance after the 1999 season. In addition to ranking second in team history with 27,141 passing yards, McNair ranks seventh in rushing yards with 3,439. After throwing for 3,215 yards, 24 **touchdowns**, and only seven interceptions in 2003, McNair was chosen as the NFL's **Most Valuable Player** (MVP).

Warren Moon
Quarterback | 1984–1993

Moon ranks 13th all-time with 49,325 passing yards for his career. He also ranks 16th all-time with 291 passing touchdowns. Moon led the league in passing yards twice during his time in Houston. He also led the league with 33 touchdown passes in 1990. The nine-time Pro Bowler is a member of the Pro Football Hall of Fame.

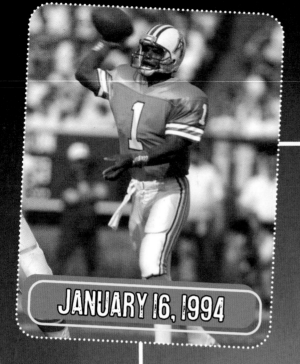

After ten seasons with the team, iconic quarterback Warren Moon plays his final game as an Oiler.

JANUARY 16, 1994

In their first game since moving to Tennessee from Houston, Texas, the team defeats the Oakland Raiders 24–21.

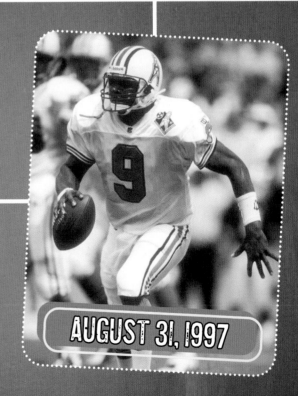

AUGUST 31, 1997

BIG DAYS

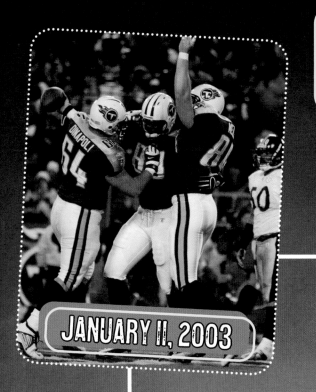

JANUARY 11, 2003

The Titans defeat the Pittsburgh Steelers 34–31 in an *overtime* playoff game thriller to advance to the AFC Championship Game.

A playoff victory over the Baltimore Ravens sets up an AFC Championship Game matchup with the Kansas City Chiefs.

JANUARY 11, 2020

MODERN-DAY MARVELS

A. J. Brown
Wide Receiver | Debut: 2019

The Titans selected Brown in the second round of the 2019 NFL Draft after a strong college career at the University of Mississippi. He totaled more than 1,000 yards in each of his first two pro seasons. After finishing 2020 with 1,075 yards and 11 touchdowns, Brown was selected for his first Pro Bowl.

Kevin Byard
Safety | Debut: 2016

In 2017, in his second pro season, Byard tied for the NFL lead with eight interceptions. That year, he was chosen for his first Pro Bowl. No player had more interceptions than Byard's 17 from 2017 through 2019. In 2020, Byard led the Titans with 111 tackles. After leading the team in tackles and interceptions in 2021, Byard was chosen for his second Pro Bowl.

Derrick Henry
Running Back | Debut: 2016

Henry led the NFL in rushing yards and touchdowns in both 2019 and 2020. He's one of the league's larger running backs and uses his power to wear down defenses over the course of a game. In 2020, he became the eighth player in NFL history to rush for more than 2,000 yards in a season.

Ryan Tannehill
Offensive Tackle | Debut: 2019

Tannehill began his career with the Miami Dolphins but came to Tennessee in a 2019 trade. In three years with the Titans, Tannehill has led the team to a 30–13 record as a starter and three-straight trips to the playoffs. He was chosen for his first Pro Bowl after the 2019 season.

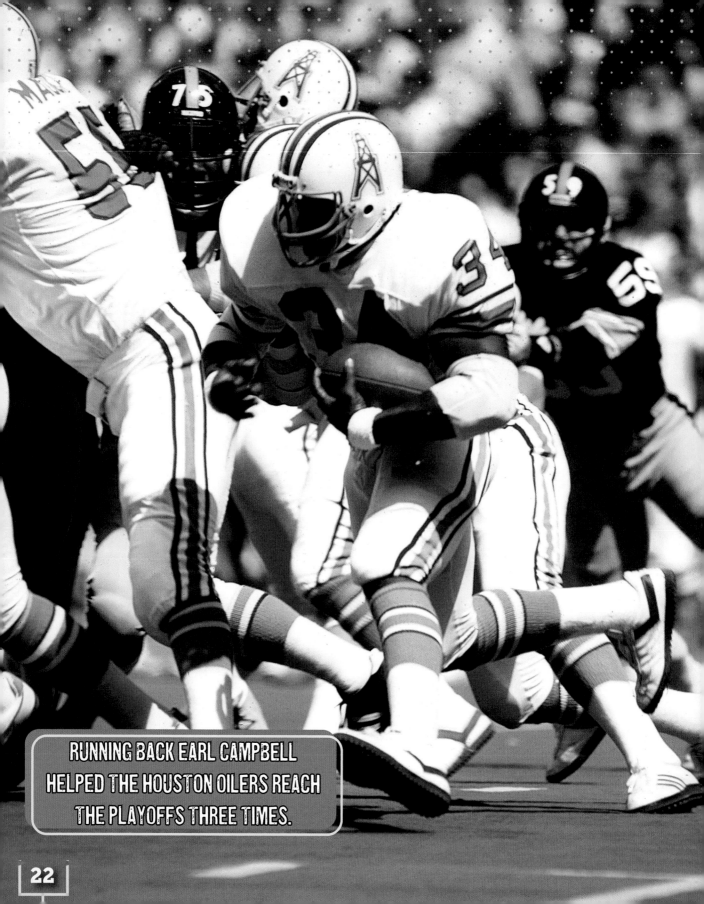

RUNNING BACK EARL CAMPBELL HELPED THE HOUSTON OILERS REACH THE PLAYOFFS THREE TIMES.

THE GOAT

EARL CAMPBELL

Campbell was the most dominant offensive force in all of football during his first three seasons. He led the league in rushing yards each year from 1978 to 1980. Campbell also led the league in rushing touchdowns in 1979 and 1980. He was voted the NFL's MVP after the 1979 season. He was selected for five Pro Bowls. Campbell is a member of the Pro Football Hall of Fame.

FAN FAVORITE

Ernest Givins–Wide Receiver
1986–1994

#1

Givins finished his career with the Oilers in Houston with 7,935 receiving yards. That's the most in team history. He was also chosen for two Pro Bowls, one of them in 1992 when he finished with ten touchdown catches. But Givins may be most beloved by fans for his "Electric Slide" touchdown dance, which became a crowd favorite at Oilers games.

THE BIG GAME

Coming into their AFC Championship Game with the Jacksonville Jaguars, the Titans had never before earned a trip to the Super Bowl. The Titans fell behind the Jaguars in the second quarter and went into halftime down 14–10. But Tennessee owned the second half. Behind a pair of rushing touchdowns from quarterback Steve McNair, the Titans scored 23 points in a row. They defeated Jacksonville 33–14. With the win, the Titans secured a spot in Super Bowl 34. Their opponent in the big game would be the St. Louis Rams.

DEFENSIVE END JEVON KEARSE
REGISTERED 14.5 SACKS DURING THE
1999 REGULAR SEASON, EARNING
HIMSELF A PRO BOWL SELECTION.

25

JEFF FISHER COACHED THE TEAM TO 142 REGULAR SEASON VICTORIES FROM 1994 TO 2010.

AMAZING FEATS

4,690 Passing Yards

In 1991 by **QUARTERBACK** Warren Moon

2,027 Rushing Yards

In 2020 by **RUNNING BACK** Derrick Henry

19 Rushing Touchdowns

In 1979 for **RUNNING BACK** Earl Campbell

1,746 Receiving Yards

In 1961 for **WIDE RECEIVER** Charley Hennigan

ALL-TIME BEST

PASSING YARDS

Warren Moon
33,685

Steve McNair
27,141

George Blanda
19,149

RUSHING YARDS

Eddie George
10,009

Earl Campbell
8,574

Chris Johnson
7,965

RECEIVING YARDS

Ernest Givins
7,935

Drew Hill
7,477

Ken Burrough
6,906

SACKS*

Elvin Bethea
105

Ray Childress
75.5

Jesse Baker
66

SCORING

Al Del Greco
1,060

Rob Bironas
1,032

George Blanda
598

INTERCEPTIONS

Jim Norton
45

Cris Dishman
31

Fred Glick
30

*unofficial before 1982

CHRIS JOHNSON'S 2009 SEASON WAS ONE OF THE BEST EVER FOR A RUNNING BACK. HE FINISHED WITH 2,006 RUSHING YARDS AND 14 RUSHING TOUCHDOWNS.

GLOSSARY

division (dih-VIZSH-un): a group of teams within the NFL that play each other more frequently and compete for the best record

Hall of Fame (HAHL of FAYM): a museum in Canton, Ohio, that honors the best players in NFL history

league (LEEG): an organization of sports teams that compete against each other

Most Valuable Player (MOHST VAL-yuh-bul PLAY-uhr): a yearly award given to the top player in the NFL

overtime (OH-vuhr-tym): extra time that is played when teams are tied at the end of four quarters

playoffs (PLAY-ahfs): a series of games after the regular season that decides which two teams play in the Super Bowl

Pro Bowl (PRO BOWL): the NFL's All-Star game where the best players in the league compete

stadium (STAY-dee-um): a building with a field and seats for fans where teams play

Super Bowl (SOO-puhr BOWL): the championship game of the NFL, played between the winners of the AFC and the NFC

touchdown (TUTCH-down): a play in which the ball is brought into the other team's end zone, resulting in six points

IN THE LIBRARY

Bulgar, Beth and Mark Bechtel. *My First Book of Football.*
New York, NY: Time Inc. Books, 2015.

Jacobs, Greg. *The Everything Kids' Football Book, 7th Edition*.
Avon, MA: Adams Media, 2021.

Sports Illustrated Kids. *The Greatest Football Teams of All Time*.
New York, NY: Time Inc. Books, 2018.

Wyner, Zach. *Tennessee Titans*. New York, NY: AV2 Books, 2020.

ON THE WEB

Visit our website for links about the Tennessee Titans:
childsworld.com/links

Note to parents, teachers, and librarians: We routinely verify our web links to make sure they are safe and active sites. Encourage your readers to check them out!

ABOUT THE AUTHOR

Josh Anderson has published over 50 books for children and young adults. His two boys are the greatest joys in his life. Hobbies include coaching his sons in youth basketball, no-holds-barred games of Apples to Apples, and taking long family walks. His favorite NFL team is a secret he'll never share!